Be

Many thanks to Berwick Ramblers
for their companionship on the
112 miles of walks described
in these pages. Particular thanks to
Maggie, Tom and the other Arthur
and to Margaret for making my tea.

Berwick Walks

twenty-four walks
within a twelve mile
radius of Berwick.

Written and illustrated
by Arthur Wood.

published by Berwick Ramblers

Published by Berwick Ramblers
5 Quay Walls, Berwick-upon-Tweed.
TD15 1HB.
published 2003   second impression 2006.
Written and illustrated by Arthur Wood.

The sketch maps are based on O.S.
Explorer Maps and are reproduced by
permission of Ordnance Survey
on behalf of the Controller of Her
Majesty's Stationery Office,
© Crown Copyright.   100040947.

ISBN: 0-9545331-0-0

Printed in Great Britain by Martins the Printers,
Sea View Works, Spittal, Berwick-upon-Tweed, TD15 1RS.
www.martins-the-printers.com

Contents

Starting points of walks

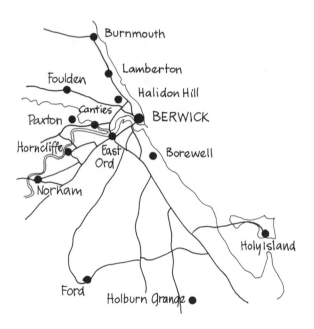

Burnmouth

Lamberton

Foulden

Halidon Hill

Canties

BERWICK

Paxton

Horncliffe

East Ord

Borewell

Norham

Holy Island

Ford

Holburn Grange

Introduction

You can glance at Berwick from the train, or drive through it in a few minutes and think you have seen it all, but set out on foot and Berwick will reveal itself to you.

The town is perched on the very top of England, but for 300 years it was an independent burgh. Before that it changed hands thirteen times, having originally been a Royal Scottish Burgh.

Because the border cuts across Berwick's hinterland, walks in both countries are included, with some outings crossing and re-crossing the border line. The walks are arranged in four sections representing the main elements of our beautiful landscape.

Quay Walls, Berwick

TOWN – Berwick is unique, lying between two countries which fought over it for hundreds of years. The Edwardian Walls are 700 years old and the Elizabethan Ramparts, started in 1558, are still virtually intact. The walk round the full circuit is unequalled in Britain.

Inside the walls the red pantiled buildings are tightly packed, rising in layers from the waterfront.

RIVER – The Tweed is a famous salmon river and seals can often be spotted in the estuary in search of a meal. Further up the river is wide and majestic with swans, herons and waterfowl.

COUNTRY – The countryside is beautiful in all seasons. It is a place of stunning vistas, wide horizons and big skies. History awaits you round most corners.

COAST— To the north of Berwick the coast is rocky and impressive, to the south there are stretches of golden beach—"the lordly strand of Northumberland." Castle ruins punctuate the horizon and sea birds wheel overhead.

Most of the town walks are regularly used for health walks. Berwick Walking for Health promotes a healthy life style. Pages 11 and 12 carry its message.

Each walk description has a sketch map, which, with the text is sufficient to enable you to follow the route. Some people find it useful to take the Ordnance Survey map as well, in case of problems and because it gives more information about the surrounding area.

An estimated time is given for each walk. The rate of travel is quite modest, allowing for stopping to look, taking a few photos, bird spotting, having a snack and generally enjoying the outing.

The Country Code lists the guiding principles for the well-mannered walker.

Weather in the area can be changeable and there is a section advising suitable equipment.

A note about foreign plants is included. One plant is particularly unpleasant.

There is information about public transport and a page listing local and official names for well-known landmarks.

It is believed that the information given is correct, but changes can occur in the countryside. No responsibility is accepted by the author or the publisher for errors or omissions, or for any loss or injury howsoever caused. You must be the judge of your own fitness, competence and experience.

the sluice, New Mills

BERWICK WALKING for health

Step out from your doorstep... Stride into health

Berwick Health Walks follow routes described in the early pages of the book. Some short routes appear elsewhere which will provide a change of routine.

Why walk ?

Being physically active is very important. Just 30 minutes of moderate activity a day, such as brisk walking, can bring a whole range of health benefits.

PLUS...

- ♥ It's free.
- ♥ Almost everyone can do it.
- ♥ You can do it on your own or with friends.
- ♥ You can do it anytime.
- ♥ You don't need special equipment.
- ♥ There is very little risk of injury.
- ♥ You can do it at your own pace.

So take those first steps, but remember... 'brisk' walking means walking so that you:

- ♥ Breathe a little faster,
- ♥ Feel a little warmer,
- ♥ Have a slightly faster heart beat.

It doesn't need to be hard work and you should still be able to talk.

START SLOWLY AND BUILD UP GRADUALLY.

The benefits of walking are:

- ♡ A lower risk of heart disease
- ♡ More energy
- ♡ Greater stamina
- ♡ Stronger bones
- ♡ Better posture
- ♡ Stronger, toned muscles
- ♡ Improved confidence

Walking is a sure and safe way to improve health but remember safety first:

- ♡ Do build up gently if you are unfit
- ♡ It doesn't have to hurt
- ♡ Make sure you can be seen walking at night
- ♡ Wear loose, comfortable clothing
- ♡ Wear appropriate footwear
- ♡ In sunny weather wear a hat
- ♡ Be careful crossing roads
- ♡ Don't walk if you feel unwell
- ♡ Stop walking if you feel sick or are in pain
- ♡ If symptoms persist seek medical help.

walking
the way
to health

British Heart Foundation

New Opportunities Fund
funded

WITH **KIA** CARS

The
Countryside
Agency

Northumberland **NHS**
Care Trust

BERWICK
UPON·TWEED
BOROUGH COUNCIL

12

Maps

All sketch maps have North at the top of the page, except the Chain Bridge Loop which has West at the top.

The walks described in the book are covered by the following Ordnance Survey Explorer Maps (orange covers).

number 340 - Holy Island and Bamburgh.

number 346 - Berwick-upon-Tweed

number 339 - Kelso, Coldstream and Lower Tweed valley.

Path Problems

Any difficulties encountered on rights of way can be reported to—

Northumberland County Council, tel.- 01670-5 33000, ask for countryside service.   *

Scottish Borders Council Ranger Service, * tel.- 01835-830281.

* Be sure you know which country the problem is in before you ring.

The Country Code

- Enjoy the Countryside and respect its life and work.

- Leave all gates as you find them.

- Use stiles when provided.

- Do not damage fences, hedges and walls.

- Keep to paths across farmland.

- Leave livestock, crops and machinery alone.

- Keep dogs under close control.

- Guard against all risk of fire.

- Help to keep all water clean.

- Take your litter home.

- Protect wildlife, plants and trees.

- Take special care on country roads. Face oncoming traffic.

Be prepared

Berwick's weather can be changeable. The forecasts never seem to cover this area, so it pays to be prepared for anything.

Unless the weather is set fair and your walk is short, take a waterproof. A spare warm garment is useful and in winter a hat and gloves are necessary.

Paths can be rough and stony or wet and muddy, so good footwear is important. Stout trainers will suffice for shorter walks, but where rough terrain is expected boots will give you ankle support. They will also keep your feet dry.

Cafés and watering holes are few and far between, so take food and a warm drink if you are going out for a half day or a whole day.

Binoculars can be useful for nature study. A compass is handy if you are familiar with its use.

Carry all your gear in a small rucksack or day sack. It leaves your hands free for pointing out interesting things to your companions.

Information

Berwick Tourist Information Centre,
106 Marygate, Berwick-upon-Tweed,
TD 15 1BN.
tel. – 01289 – 330733 .
e.mail – tourism @ berwick-upon-tweed.gov.uk

Eyemouth Visitor Information Centre,
the Auld Kirk, Manse Road, Eyemouth,
TD 14 5JE.
tel. – 018907 – 50678.
e.mail – eyemouth @ scot-borders.co.uk

Local Transport

Berwick's bus service is operated by five companies. There is no comprehensive timetable and services leave from different parts of the town.
Ask the T.I.C. for details of a particular service and where it starts from.

The Eyemouth Travel Guide lists all bus services in the Eyemouth area.

Foreign Invaders

Giant Hogweed -
HERACLEUM
 MANTEGAZZIANUM -
was brought to Britain
by Victorian botanists
from the Caucasus.
It grows 12 feet (3.6M)
tall, with coarse deeply
cut leaves, fluted stems
and large white flower
heads.
The sap photosensitises
the skin, causing large
water blisters.
Children are attracted
to the hollow stems.
Bad cases require
medical help.
KEEP CLEAR OF THIS
PLANT.

Other strangers —
Japanese Knotweed,
dense thickets, 6 feet
(2M) high.
Himalayan Balsam,
5 feet (1.5M), fleshy leaves,
pink flowers. Clogs
river banks and
footpaths occasionally.

What is it called?

Many places in Berwick have two names – a local one and an official one. The local names have been used in the walk descriptions, so that you will have more success if you have to ask the way.

the Old Bridge —— Berwick Bridge
the New Bridge —— Royal Tweed Bridge
the Railway Bridge —— Royal Border Bridge
the High Street —————————— Marygate
the Town Hall —————— the Guild Hall
the Walls —— Elizabethan Ramparts
the New Road ———————— Riverside Walk
the Parish Church —— Holy Trinity Church
Canties Bridge —— Whiteadder Bridge
Chain Bridge —— Union Chain Bridge

Town Walks

the Ramparts

Berwick's Ramparts are uniquely intact and they offer a
remarkable, traffic free, introduction to the old town.
The circuit is 1·3 miles (2·1 km.) and for generations the
townsfolk have taken their constitutional there. It can
be walked in half an hour or enjoyed at a more leisurely
pace.

Start the walk at Bridge End, where the Old Bridge
leaves Berwick. Facing the town Hall Spire, go right,
cross the road and take the level footpath along
the Edwardian Walls. The stone paved walkway
has Georgian terraced houses on the left and a
stout parapet on the right. Openings at Sallyport
and Sandgate give unexpected views into the old
town with its famous red roofs. Beyond the
Customs House and the home of Thomas Sword
Good, the painter, the route widens out and passes
the three imposing houses of Wellington Terrace.
On the right is Coxon's Tower. Steps to the top
offer good views upstream to the three bridges and
down the estuary to Spittal. The Walls bend round
to the left, with gun ports in the parapet. At Fishers
Fort lies a Russian cannon captured in the Crimea.

The path passes over Nessgate, through a metal gate and up Kipper Hill. This is the start of the Elizabethan Ramparts, built to an Italian design as defence against cannon. Huge projecting bastions at the corners provided raking crossfire along the face of the curtain walls. The fortifications were never used against an enemy.

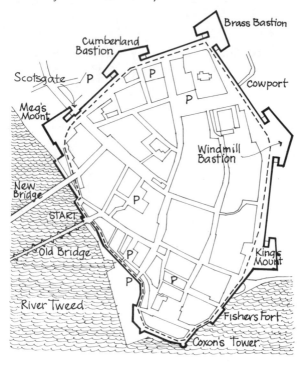

The first bastion, Kings Mount, is on the right at the top of Kipper Hill. As the route continues there are two paths, a lower secure one and an upper path close to the wallhead. Walkers are advised to use the lower path which is much safer. Children and dogs should be closely supervised. Soon a flight of steps is reached leading   down to a swing park and giving an opportunity to view the ramparts from the attacker's point of view.

Next
comes Windmill Bastion, worth climbing up for good views out to sea and back into town. The path passes Berwick Barracks which now houses the Borough Museum and passes over Cowport, the only original gateway. At a sharp corner lies Brass Bastion and to the left Holy Trinity Church, built during the Protectorate, it lacks a steeple and a bell.

COWPORT

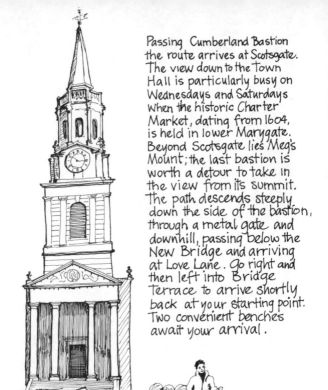

Passing Cumberland Bastion the route arrives at Scotsgate. The view down to the Town Hall is particularly busy on Wednesdays and Saturdays when the historic Charter Market, dating from 1604, is held in lower Marygate. Beyond Scotsgate lies Meg's Mount; the last bastion is worth a detour to take in the view from its summit. The path descends steeply down the side of the bastion, through a metal gate and downhill, passing below the New Bridge and arriving at Love Lane. Go right and then left into Bridge Terrace to arrive shortly back at your starting point. Two convenient benches await your arrival.

BERWICK'S CHARTER MARKET

"We grant that the mayor, bailiffs and burgesses of the burgh – may forever have, hold and keep – two markets weekly." James VI & I, April 1604.

the New Road

Bridge End

The New Road is the local name for the
riverside path, upstream from the Old Bridge.
It was built during the Depression following
the Napoleonic Wars, so it isn't exactly new.
The walk along to Letham Plantation and
back is 2 miles (3km), but there are several
variations described in the text. The riverside
path is paved, but there is no edge protection
and walkers should take care where there
is a drop to the water.

  Start at Bridge End and, with your back to
the river, go left along Bridge Terrace, turning
right to the foot of Bankhill. The signpost –
Tweed Footpath – directs you along the
level path, passing below the New Bridge,
then downhill with Berwick Amateur Rowing
Club on the left. The riverside walk now
stretches ahead with the great sweep of
the Railway Bridge closing the view.

Designed by Robert Stephenson, the bridge was opened in 1850 by Queen Victoria. Just before the Railway Bridge a flight of steps goes up to the right, leading to Castle Vale Park and the railway station.

Beyond the Railway Bridge the path disappears into a low passage below the Castle Water Tower, emerging into daylight after passing dark openings with metal barred gates.

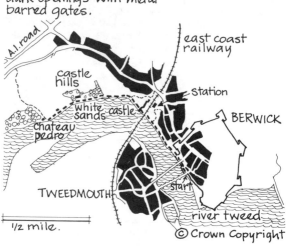

A.1. road

east coast railway

castle hills

station

white sands

castle

BERWICK

chateau pedro

TWEEDMOUTH

start

½ mile.

river tweed

© Crown Copyright

26

It is possible to
explore the upper
floor of the tower
with its gun embrasures.
The path is now
closer to water level.
Swans are often to
be seen and at low
tide solitary herons
stand patiently
waiting for their

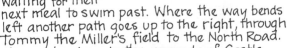

next meal to swim past. Where the way bends
left another path goes up to the right, through
Tommy the Miller's field to the North Road.
  Trees ahead are in the grounds of Castle
Hills, formerly a maternity home. The
small white building you next pass is
Whitesands Salmon Fishing Shiel, now
disused.

Just before the bungalow, called
Chateau Pedro, another path
goes up to the right. This is
Askew's Walk, a sometimes
muddy path, but always a
charming walk up the side
of the plantation. Arriving
at the road turn right to come
on to Castle Terrace, where
another right turn will bring
you back down into town.
                Alternatively
when you reach Chateau
Pedro you can return along
the New Road. The walk is
often sheltered when the rest
of the town is windy, and the
views are always interesting.

Magdalene Fields

This walk visits the medieval fortifications, the coast and the river estuary. It is 2·6 miles (4·2 km.) long and takes just over an hour at a brisk pace. Most of the route is paved, but there is a grass path along the cliff top. Walkers should be aware of golfers round the golf course, but the danger of flying balls is minimal because the fairways are generally parallel to the route.

The walk can be superb on a fine warm day and 'bracing' in a storm.

Start at Bridge End and, with your back to the river, go left along Bridge Terrace, turning right to the foot of Bankhill. Take the uphill path, going under the New Bridge (1927) and passing the statue of

Lady Jerningham, which gazes towards
her home, Longridge Towers. The road curves
round to the right and arrives at Marygate.
Go through the Scotsgate arch and up
Castlegate to cross at the pedestrian
crossing. Continue uphill and where it
levels out keep right of the war memorial,
turning right into a short cul-de-sac.
At the foot take a cobbled path on your left.
Turning right into High Greens, go down
the road to the letter box and turn left up
a narrow path leading to the Bell Tower.
Built to warn of marauding Scots, the tower
sits on the medieval walls, now mostly
grassy mounds.

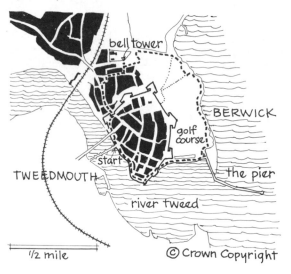

bell tower

BERWICK

golf course

start

the pier

TWEEDMOUTH

river tweed

1/2 mile

© Crown Copyright

Go right, before the tower, along a flat grassy path and as you reach the end there is an opportunity to go up left to visit Lords Mount. The ruin was excavated in 1970 revealing much of the Henry VIII masonry. The fort was superseded soon after its completion by the Elizabethan Ramparts.

Back on the path, go through the wall and down some old worn steps to follow the road round to the left. On reaching the entrance sign for Berwick Holiday Centre turn right towards the sea. Do not go down the road, but follow the path on the far side of a long hollow. It is Spades Mire, a defensive ditch that predates the medieval walls.

The path skirts parked caravans and eventually arrives at the coast and a public convenience. Keep on, following the tarmac path and at a junction go left, then right on to the grass alongside the cliff-top fence. Below you, when the tide is out, are curving limestone reefs and many rock pools.

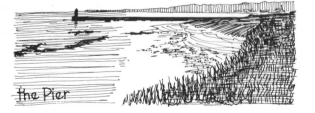

the Pier

quay walls

Follow the fence, keeping an eye on golfers, until you reach two cast iron posts. Go between them and follow the road downhill, curving right. On level grass to the left is the recently restored 'Lowry Shelter' (see the Lowry Trail.)

Now between high walls, the road curves to the right, coming on to Pier Road, with Berwick Pier stretching away to the left and the Tweed Estuary in front. Swans are often seen in stately procession.

There is no edge protection on Pier Road, so it is prudent to keep to the right hand side of the road. After passing through Nessgate turn left onto the Walls, following the path past Fisher's Fort, Coxon's Tower and Wellington Terrace, back along Quay Walls to the Old Bridge and your starting point.

Askew's Walk

  This walk follows the river upstream, climbs
a woodside path and comes back into town
on quiet roads. It is 3 miles (5km) in length
and can be walked in an hour and a half,
mostly on paved paths. In former times
Askew's Walk was a popular Sunday
afternoon's walk.
  Start at Bridge End and, with your back
to the river, go left along Bridge Terrace,
turning right to the foot of Bankhill. The
signpost- Tweed Footpath- directs you
along the level path, passing below the
New Bridge, then downhill to the New
Road.
  On the right you pass Conqueror's Well,
a drinking fountain named after a

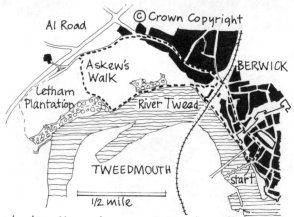

nineteenth century watchmaker. There is
a significant drop from path level to the river,
so walkers should beware of the hazard.

Birdlife is always plentiful on the river
bank. Berwick's famous swans are
invariably present, gulls often wheel and
turn overhead and solitary herons stand
quietly in the distance.

Passing below the Railway Bridge, the
walker arrives at the Castle Water Tower.
A low dark passage, with mysterious
openings on each side, leads through the
tower. Emerging into the light, the path
can be seen stretching round the water's
edge past the trees of Castle Hills to
Letham Plantation.

Seats at the pathside offer a resting place
on warm days.

Beyond the Castle Hills trees lies White Sands Fishing Shiel, now disused. Until a few years ago salmon fishing had been carried on since early Medieval times. Boats, called cobbles, were rowed out dropping the hang net in a semi-circle. The net was then pulled in, hopefully enclosing the salmon.

Arriving at the plantation, and just before the bungalow, Chateau Pedro, a fingerpost points up a narrow path, which is Askew's Walk. The surface can be muddy at times, but it improves higher up and the walker is rewarded with a delightful woodside path, curving and twisting upwards.

Coming out on to the road, turn right, uphill and walk along to Castle Terrace. To the South there are views to the Cheviot Hills. Turn right, down Castle Terrace, a pleasant road of substantial houses built at the dawn of the 20th. century. Follow the pavement, crossing over to the other side where it stops.

At the foot of Castle Terrace you can go through a gate on the right and down Tommy the Miller's Field to the New Road, or you can continue over the railway into Castlegate and back into Berwick.

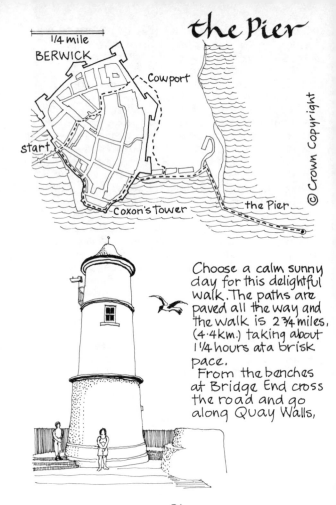

the Pier

1/4 mile
BERWICK

Cowport

start

Coxon's Tower

the Pier

© Crown Copyright

Choose a calm sunny day for this delightful walk. The paths are paved all the way and the walk is 2¾ miles. (4.4km.) taking about 1¼ hours at a brisk pace.

From the benches at Bridge End cross the road and go along Quay Walls,

36

passing the terraced Georgian houses.
Beyond Coxon's Tower and the Russian
cannon on Fisher's Fort go down and
through Nessgate.

There is a wide panorama accross the
estuary to Spittal Point and round to
the Pier. Follow Pier Road round to the
left, keeping away from the unprotected
edge, and walking along to the pier. In
stormy weather waves break over the
Pier and Lighthouse. You should only go
there on calm days.

Built to protect the harbour, the Pier
dates from 1821. It replaced Queen
Elizabeth's Pier. At the first corner is
Crabwater, a stone-built fishing batt,
where walkers would watch the salmon
fishers. Crabwater is no longer used.
Also at the corner are navigation lights,
for ships negotiating the tortuous river
channel.

On a good day grey seals come up for
breath as they hunt for salmon. Often
eider ducks can be seen. Locally they are
called "Cuddy Ducks", from their association
with St. Cuthbert on the Farne Islands.

At the end of the Pier is the Lighthouse,
painted red and white. The light is
automatic, so it is no longer manned.

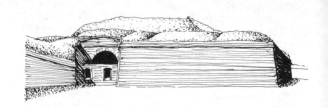

Brass Bastion

Coming back you are rewarded with a mariner's view of Berwick, with Halidon Hill beyond. Return along Pier Road and just before the tentmaker's building go up a long flight of steps on the right.

At the top, when you have got your breath back, go left and follow the path as it runs outside the Elizabethan Ramparts. Pass Windmill Bastion and go through a gate, turning left to Cowport. The grassed area with goal posts is the Stanks, with Brass Bastion beyond

Through Cowport, continue across the grass area in front of the Barracks and carry on to Church Street. Turn left here, going down to Chapel Street coming in from the right. Cross diagonally and go down Crawford's Alley to Marygate. Cross and continue down West Street to find Bridge End.

Back Lanes of Spittal and Tweedmouth

A walk round the quiet back lanes of Spittal and Tweedmouth giving spectacular views of Berwick Walls, the Pier and the Tweed Estuary. Mostly on paved paths, it is an easy walk of 4·75 miles (7·6km), taking two hours of brisk walking.

Start at the Tweedmouth end of the Old Bridge and go right, under the New Bridge. Cross the road and walk through the West End, past the Thatch Inn, with its rider's mounting block. Pass Kingdom Hall, turning left at West End Road and

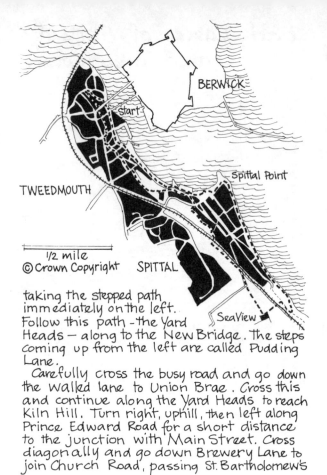

BERWICK

Start

Spittal Point

TWEEDMOUTH

½ mile
© Crown Copyright

SPITTAL

SeaView

taking the stepped path
immediately on the left.
Follow this path – the Yard
Heads — along to the New Bridge. The steps
coming up from the left are called Pudding
Lane.

Carefully cross the busy road and go down
the walled lane to Union Brae. Cross this
and continue along the Yard Heads to reach
Kiln Hill. Turn right, uphill, then left along
Prince Edward Road for a short distance
to the junction with Main Street. Cross
diagonally and go down Brewery Lane to
join Church Road, passing St. Bartholomew's

Church on your left. The churchyard contains the tombstone of John Mackay Wilson, author of 'Tales of the Border' and sometime editor of the Berwick Advertiser.

Go left and right into Well Square, keeping to the right, up Well Road and emerging on to Mount Road. Go diagonally left across the road and up steps to the right leading to the Goodie Patchie. Continue along this well surfaced path ignoring turnings to the left and right until you pass over the old railway viaduct. Admire the view across the estuary of Berwick's red roofed houses gathered round the Town Hall, with Ramparts protecting the shore line.

Steps lead down to Dock Road. Follow this to the right for a few yards and take

another path on the right. You are now in Spittal and soon the path arrives at Billendean Road. Cross carefully because downhill traffic comes round the corner quickly.

Go right to more steps and a narrow path between walls – the Bank Heads. At the end go down steps and turn right, uphill, to a low foot tunnel under

the East Coast Railway Line. Climb the steps
and turn left along an unsurfaced track
parallel to the railway. Join Cow Road at the
level crossing and continue for 200 yards.
At the corner keep straight on along a
roughly surfaced track to Sea View Farm.
The views of Berwick Bay and down to
Holy Island are stunning.

Follow the road round to the left and
downhill under the railway line. Coming
on to the coastal path turn right and
continue to a stepped path on the left leading
down to Spittal Promenade. Follow the Prom
towards Spittal Point, passing the Amusement
Pavilion, with refreshments and public
conveniences (round the back).

Follow the path round Spittal Point and
go left down Sandstell Road. Go diagonally
across the car park and head for
Dock Road. Walk towards Tweedmouth,
passing the Stone Quay and Carr Rock
Jetty. Continue on the grass verge to the Dock,
following Main Street to the Old Bridge.

Berwick's Lowry Trail

1/4 mile

① Dewar's Lane
② Palace Street
③ the Pier
④ the Sea
⑤ on the Sands
⑥ the Lions
⑦ Football Match
⑧ the Town Hall
⑨ Strother's Yard
⑩ Bridge End
⑪ Sally Port

BERWICK

©Crown Copyright — the Pier

L.S.Lowry (1887–1976) visited the town from the mid-1930's until the summer before he died. The trail connects the sites of his finest paintings and drawings. Information boards are displayed at each site.

> The Lowry Trail Leaflet is available from the Tourist Information Centre. For more details of the work of Lowry in Berwick look for the book by Edwin Bowes in bookshops.

The trail starts at Dewar's Lane ①. Go down the lane, with its whin setts, and turn left at the foot, passing below a building to come out into the car park.

Carry straight on, crossing Sandgate, into Palace Street ②. Bear round right, then left, passing the Main Guard, then a house with a bust of Wellington over the door.

Coming up onto the Walls, go left past Fisher's Fort with it's Russian cannon and at Nessgate go down and through to Pier Road. The next viewpoint ③ the Pier, is on the small grass area on the right.

Go along Pier Road and, if the weather is calm, go along the Pier to ④, the Sea. In stormy weather there is a danger of being swept off by waves.

Returning from the lighthouse go round behind the Pier to ⑤. The beach shelter was restored by the Berwick Preservation Trust in 2001.

Continue along the tarmac road which bears left uphill. At the top cross the car park and find the path passing the Coastguard houses and Devon Terrace, continuing through parkland to the foot of the Ramparts. An opening in the Walls contains a flight of steps to the wall top.

Turning right along the Walls path, the prominent house away to the left is the Lions House, ⑥ which Lowry may have thought of buying.

The airy Ramparts path leads past Ravensdowne Barracks and opposite the Parish Church, below the Walls, is the Stanks. ⑦

Continuing on the Walls, the view from Scotsgate gives a splendid glimpse of Marygate and the Town Hall, ⑧.

At this point an excursion down Marygate to Strother's Yard, ⑨, gives you the chance of a cup of tea.

The next site, Bridge End, ⑩, is accessible via West Street from Strother's Yard, or from Scotsgate by continuing down Bankhill, below the New Bridge.

From Bridge End go down the rough cobbled slope to the Quayside to find the low, narrow opening to Sallyport, ⑪.

This is the end of the Berwick section, but there is more across the river, which can occupy an afternoon, or another day.

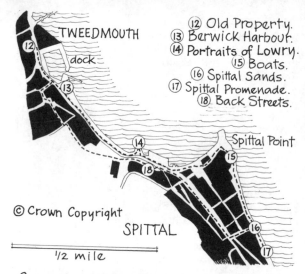

TWEEDMOUTH

dock

⑫ Old Property.
⑬ Berwick Harbour.
⑭ Portraits of Lowry.
⑮ Boats.
⑯ Spittal Sands.
⑰ Spittal Promenade.
⑱ Back Streets.

Spittal Point

© Crown Copyright

SPITTAL

½ mile

Cross the Old Bridge to Tweedmouth, turning left along Main Street to ⑫, the recessed houses. Carry on past Tweed Dock to a wide grass verge, ⑬, then along to Carr Rock Jetty, ⑭. Approaching Spittal, go left before the fish preparation works, cross the car park and go along Sandstell Road to Spittal Point ⑮ Follow the path round, right, coming down onto the reconstructed Promenade, ⑯, ⑰. The Amusements Pavilion has limited refreshments and Public Conveniences round the back.

The return to Berwick can be achieved by retracing your steps, or you can go along Sea Road into Main Street, turning right and walking along past the spire of St. Paul's Church. Cross Princes Street and after a short distance go up steps on the left to a path which gives splendid views of Berwick and the bridges, particularly from the short viaduct.⑱ The continuing path is called the Goodie Patchie and it comes out, down steps, onto Mount Road. Go left, cross the road and go down, right, into Well Square. Pass Tweedmouth Parish Church (Saint Bartholomew's) and follow round, right, to Dock Road, turning left to retrace your steps back to the Old Bridge.

Spittal Point

River Walks

Horncliffe Walk

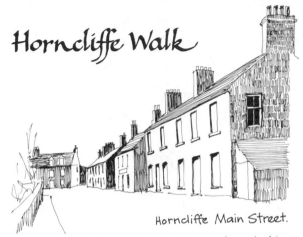

Horncliffe Main Street.

A peaceful riverside stroll, a unique bridge and a honey farm. The walk is half on grass and half on roads. It is 3 miles (4.5km) and takes about two hours. There is a bus service to Horncliffe.

Go along Main Street turning left into the Square. At the far end go between the last two houses turning sharp right, up a track with a swing park on the right. The small brick building is a public toilet. Keep straight on and go through a kissing gate following the path to go down steps to a track. Go left down the track turning right along the banks of the River Tweed past a fishing shiel.

The path follows a long right hand bend in the river, first on top of a

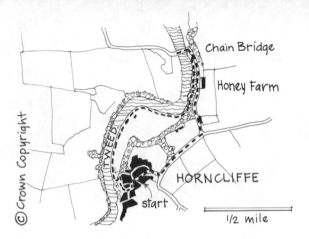

Chain Bridge

Honey Farm

HORNCLIFFE

start

1/2 mile

flood bank and through a wicket gate,
then on more level ground. Pass the
ruin of a fishing shiel and carry on as
the river bends left.

On this quiet stretch of river you will
often see herons flying lazily along the
far bank, while nervous mallards
scuttle noisily away.

Make for a gate at the end of a small
footbridge and continue to a second
gate. The path now wanders among
bankside trees, with an occasional
fallen branch to clamber over.

At length the path goes up to the road
near Chain Bridge. Follow the road down
and cross the bridge, passing into Scotland
at the mid point. This was the first
suspension bridge in Europe to carry

road traffic. An information board gives the history of the bridge.

To return to Horncliffe go back across the bridge and follow the road uphill. Half way up, on the left is Chain Bridge Honey Farm, worth a visit for the informative displays and a little gentle shopping.

Continue uphill and turn right at the road junction, walking on the pavement. On the right is Horncliffe House, a Palladian mansion built about 1800. Continue on the road and turn right up into Horncliffe. The Fisher's Arms in Main Street is a good stopping point.

Chain Bridge

Paxton Circular

This walk starts in Scotland and visits England, exploring the valleys of Whiteadder Water and the Tweed. It is 7 miles (11 km) and can be walked in about 4 hours. Most of the walk is off road and conditions can be muddy underfoot, while paths can be overgrown in summer. Good footwear is essential.

Paxton has a bus service and there is a car park up Merse View.

Facing the Cross Inn go right along the road, going up the second road on the left (ignore the Private Road sign). At the top follow the road to the right and walk along to the end. A field edge path goes off to the left, turning right past the hedge. This path leads down through a wicket gate and steeply down to a footbridge over Whiteadder Water.

There are high sandstone cliffs on

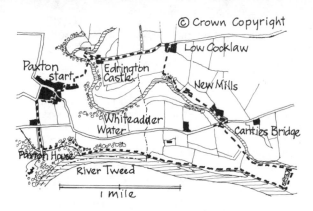

the other side and to the left Edrington
Castle Mill.

Go past the mill and look on the far
side for a stone between two first floor
windows marking the water level of the
great flood of 1948. Continue to the foot of
the hill and go sharp right up the road.

At the top, on the right, beyond the houses is all that remains of Edrington Castle. Being so close to the border both nations squabbled over it and there is only a short section of wall left.

Walk up to a road junction where the border comes down the Bound Road from the left. It continues down the overgrown track to the right, but you cannot follow it because it leads to the Whiteadder where there is no bridge. You must therefore make for Cantie's Bridge by continuing straight on to Low Cocklaw.

A fingerpost pointing right directs you through the houses. Turn right then left down mown grass to a gate into a field. Keep straight on alongside the hedge. Climb a stile into scrubby woodland, going left on a faint path which is somewhat overgrown and very narrow in places. Come down eventually to the river, drawn by the sound of the weir.

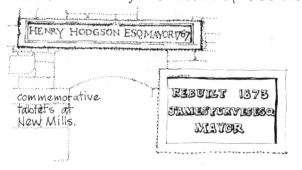

HENRY HODGSON ESQ MAYOR 1767

REBUILT 1873
JAMES PURVES ESQ
MAYOR

commemorative
tablets at
New Mills.

Climb the stile onto the sluice wall over the old mill race. Walk along the bank, going through a gate onto a rough road at New Mills. They were built by Berwick Corporation and stones on the remaining building record rebuildings in 1767 and 1873.

The track brings you past modern houses to the Corporation Arms, now a house and Canties Bridge. Cross the bridge and go down to the left to an old track leading to the river. The gate is locked, so you must climb two stiles to get past it. Continue on the track, which shadows the Whiteadder downstream. At the tree strip climb the stile and go right along the far side of the trees to reach the Tweed. Go right, upstream, passing in front of Broad Shiel and North Bells Shiel.

Broad Shiel

There are stiles at each fence line and the path can be strewn with branches left by flood water. The rough road you cross is the Bound Road again. The border runs to the centre of the Tweed and turns upstream as far as Coldstream, where it makes for the Cheviot Hills and thence to the Solway Firth.

Continue along the riverside, now in Scotland, pass two shiels and beside a stone retaining wall. Where the wall ends steps lead up to a footbridge.

Do not cross the bridge but go sharp right uphill following yellow waymarks. You are now in the grounds of Paxton House and the path winds round the edge of Linn Dean, coming out on to the driveway of Paxton House. There is a fine bridge on the left, but our route goes right, up the drive, towards the main road. Cross the road and continue towards Paxton village.

Just before a road junction take a gravel path on the right. Follow this path which turns left onto a narrow road. Go right then left, past the village water pump, going up between a wall and a house. You will recognise your starting point and the Cross Inn where you might seek refreshment.

Coroner's Meadow

THIS
WAY

   This is a pleasant walk from Canties
Bridge along the banks of Whiteadder
Water and the River Tweed. The route is
mostly on grass and it is 3·5 miles (5·5 km)
long, taking about 2 hours. The walk
starts at the far side of Canties Bridge
(on the B 6461) at a parking place down to
the left.
   Go down the old track towards the
river, climbing two stiles to get past the
locked gate. Turn left under the bridge
and walk alongside Whiteadder Water to
a clump of trees.

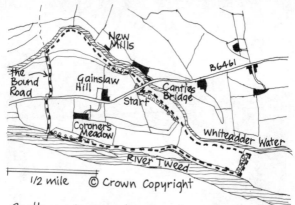

1/2 mile   © Crown Copyright

Go through the wicket gate and follow
the path as it dips down to river level.
There is a steep rise up the bank at the
far end. This section can sometimes be
flooded, but there is a higher path among
the trees. It is difficult to see, being
overgrown.

A stile brings you onto a grassy haugh
where the right of way follows the river.
The sandstone buildings on the opposite
bank are all that is left of New Mills.
They were built by Berwick Corporation
to provide flour for the town. Further
on is the weir built 300 years ago to
power the mills.

At the end of the haugh go through
a gate onto a rough track which is
part of the Bound Road. The border
runs along its centre line.

The fields or
territory of Berwick
commonly called The
Berwick Bounds
are environed and
divided from Scotland
by a notorious
boundary called
The Bound Road.

Bowes Survey 1542

Go left uphill walking in England if you
are on the left or Scotland if you choose
the right. Birdsong is all that you will
hear as the track levels out and comes to
the B6461 road at Paxton Toll. Cross
diagonally and continue on the Bound
Road as it dips down to the Tweed.
In 1550 Sir Robert Bowes surveyed the
fords of the Tweed and here he listed
Yare Ford as a major crossing.

Go left at the end of the Bound Road.
The long level grass field before you is
Coroner's Meadow, probably a grazing area
provided for the town official.

Follow the track, passing in front of
North Bells Fishing Shiel, now a weekend
retreat. Bowes noted two other fords

near here, the Over Bells and the Nether Bells. It is difficult to find their exact position.

The riverside path continues, crossing into Coroner's Meadow at the end of the trees. After a stile follow along the fence to a second stile into an overgrown field with Broad Shiel at the far end. Just beyond the Shiel the right of way turns left to follow the edge of a tree belt, bringing you to the banks of the Whiteadder.

Turn left at the end of the trees and climb the stile. Follow the tractor track along the edge of a cropped field, then cross another stile to a grass field with the river on your right. Ahead is Canties Bridge. The track goes along the foot of a bank with trees and brings you back to the starting point.

Norham Circle

Norham is a picturesque village on the banks of the Tweed with a castle and a fine church. It has a shop, a butcher, a baker, a post office, two pubs and a public convenience. There is a bus service from Berwick.

The walk takes you through the village and round the immediate country. At 4 miles (6.5km) it can be walked in a little over 2 hours. The footpaths are generally well maintained.

Start from the village cross on the green and walk towards the castle at the far end of Castle Street.

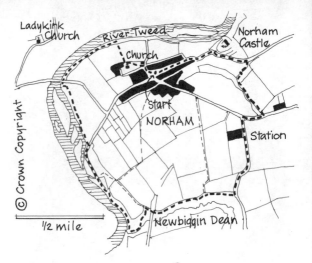

The prince bishops of Durham built the castle to control two important fords on the Tweed.

Follow the road past the castle entrance and where it bends left cross over and go through a gate where the fingerpost indicates a bridleway to Morrishall Farm. Go down the field to a gated bridge on the left. Cross the bridge and follow the path beside the stream. Go through a gate and follow the fence along to a second gate which brings you to a road. Turn right, being careful of speeding traffic coming round the bend. Go up a minor road on the left, passing Norham Station,

Old Halterburnhead

Go through the gate and take the track on the left which climbs in a zig zag to reach the col between the Curr and Black Hag. Shortly after the Pennine Way is joined at G.R.858 236. In 400 yards (G.R.861 233), shortly before the wall ahead (the Border), take the track to the right, (SE). It is not very clear at first. Initially it contours round the head of the valley of the Rowhope Burn before dropping steeply to it. Now a clear track, it follows the burn South. The track divides just after a plantation and after crossing the Alderhope Burn.

Go right, passing Auchope on the other side of the burn and continue round Fasset Hill. You will see Sourhope, the hillfarming research station, below. At the track junction take the track right, down to Sourhope. Just after passing a row of cottages on your left, take the track to your left to cross the bridge over Kaim Burn and continue on past the black barn in a southeasterly direction. The track gradually climbs along the side of Park Law. Cashmere goats are often seen in this vicinity. In about a mile from Sourhope, at G.R.859 196, take a faint quad bike track right, S, up to the col between Auchope Rig and

Bonnie Laws, to meet the fence coming down the
Rig. Go right and then through the gate on your left
and immediately through the gate in front of you.
The Track now drops down slightly east of south,
To cross the small burn on your left at a vehicle
bridge and then down the east side of Cheviot
Burn. It is not shown on the map. It soon reaches
Cocklawfoot, coming in through the farm buildings.

There are no facilities of any kind after leaving
Kirk Yetholm. There is no public transport to
Cocklawfoot and a car or pre-arranged taxi will
be necessary. Mobile phone reception is extremely
limited in the Cheviots, so do not rely on this
in making any arrangements.

If you are doing a continuous walk it is possible
to arrange accommodation at Uswayford Farm.
Follow the main route turning left at the Hexpath Gate
and dropping down to Uswayford. Next morning take
the path north from Uswayford to join Salter's Road
at GR 886155. The public road does not go to Uswayford.

Walk six
Cocklawfoot to Hartside

The Borough boundary which we are following
now leaves the national border and makes its
way through the Cheviots in an easterly
direction. Luckily there are ancient tracks,
Clennell Street and Salter's Road, which shadow
the boundary. There are no facilities en route
and no escape routes, so take everything you
will need, especially wet weather gear.

The walk is 11.25 miles (18km) and it will
take about 7 hours. There is no public
transport at either end of the walk. Map
reading and compass work will be required,
so do not attempt this walk unless you are
experienced in navigation. Check the weather
forecast and be prepared for sudden changes
in the weather.

There is parking on the roadside before
Cocklawfoot Farm. Cross the plank bridge
and go through a gate into the farmyard.
A fingerpost on the right, marked Border Ridge,
indicates your route. This is Clennell Street

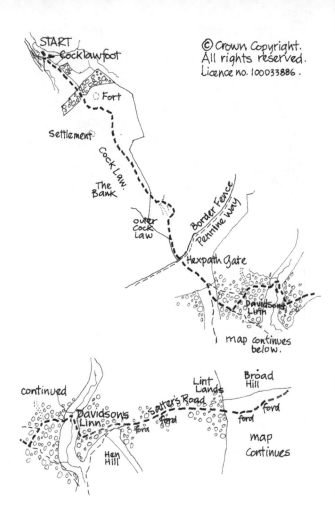

START
Cocklawfoot

○ Fort

Settlement

Cock Law

The Bank

Outer Cock Law

Border Fence
Pennine Way

Hexpath Gate

Davidsons Linn

map continues below.

continued

Davidsons Linn

Lint Lands

Broad Hill

Salter's Road

ford

ford

ford

ford

Hen Hill

map continues

69

which leads to Alwinton in the Coquet valley.
The track ahead is clear. It passes through
a stand of trees (last chance for a discreet
pee stop), before gradually climbing over Cock
Law. This is a good vantage point to view
the broad sweep of the Border Ridge from
Windy Gyle (right) to the Cheviot and the Schill (left).
Go through a gate and follow the track as it
veers left round Outer Cock Law. Note the deep
furrows on the right, worn by the many hooves
of horses and cattle through the ages.

The next gate is Hexpathgate, on the English/
Scottish border. Once through you cross the
Pennine Way, but your route goes straight
ahead. Hexpathgate was a meeting place for
Wardens of the Border Marches on truce days.
It was hereabouts that Lord Francis Russell was
murdered at one such meeting. He was the
son-in-law of Sir John Forster, warden of the
middle marches.

Follow the track, still Clennell Street, gently down hill. The first fingerpost on the left directs you along Salter's Road, but at present it is impassable through the trees due to irresponsible scrambling motorcyclists who have churned the peat into evil black porridge. You are strongly advised to continue on to a second fingerpost 200 yards further on, signed Uswayford.

The path leads down into the trees on a muddy ride. On reaching a forest track go left, looking out for a waymark on the right. Go a short distance beyond it and take an easier way into the trees, over a plank bridge. You are now on Salter's Road. Care needs to be taken for the way is narrow, with deep ruts and steep sides with slippery tree roots.

Eventually you come out of the trees on the side of the steep valley of the Usway Burn. Below you is the picturesque waterfall of Davidson's Linn — a good picnic spot. Further upstream a new footbridge takes you over the burn.

waterfall at Davidson's Linn

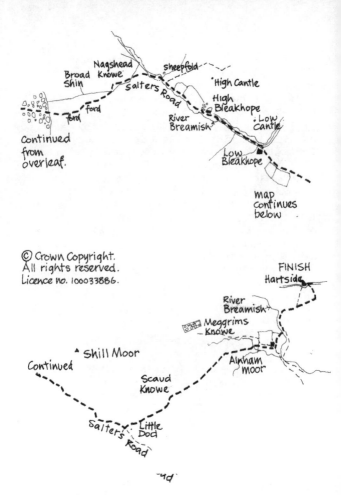

Broad Shin
Nagshead Knowe
sheepfold
Salters Road
High Cantle
High Breakhope
River Breamish
Low Cantle
ford   ford
Continued from overleaf.
Low Breakhope
map continues below

FINISH
Hartside
River Breamish
Meggrims Knowe
▲ Shill Moor
Continued
Scaud Knowe
Ainham moor
Salter's Road
Little Dod
...d

72

looking back to High Bleakhope

Go right on a path climbing towards more trees, where it widens into a track. More ruts and bogs greet you as you make your way along to another fingerpost showing Salter's Road to the left. Be careful here because it would be all too easy to continue along the forest ride which takes you to the right. Keep on the left hand track until it emerges from the trees at a gate.

Out in the open the way is less clear as it descends to the Bleakhopes. It is advisable to take compass bearings to get you downhill to the infant River Breamish. When you reach a gated fence on your left, go through and continue down towards a sheep stell and the river. Follow downstream towards High Bleakhope and walk through the farm, where the way becomes a metalled road.

In the 12th century the Cistercian monks of Newminster were granted huge areas of these hills for sheep grazing by the de Umfraville lords of Redesdale and Harbottle. They shepherded sheep here until the dissolution of the monasteries.

Low
Bleakhope

Walk on to Low Bleakhope and, where the road
bends left, continue straight on through a shallow
ford and steadily uphill. The stony path is still
Salter's Road and it leads through a gate to the
crest of a hill. The path descends and ahead of you
another small hill, Little Dod, can be seen. As you
approach it take the waymarked post on the left,
directing you down to Alnhammoor Farm and
away from Salter's Road.

At the bottom of the valley the Shank Burn
appears on the right and the path crosses a
small side stream to a steep stile. Veer right
with the path past the farmhouse, then sharp
left through a small field with wicket gates
at either end. Coming onto the road go right,
downhill and cross over the River Breamish by
the plank bridge. Turn left and stay on the
road all the way to Hartside.

Alnhammoor

walk seven
Hartside to
Powburn

heading up to Cobden

    This walk takes you from the high Cheviots down
through the foothills to the lowlands. It also takes
you from the Bronze and Iron Ages to the Roman
occupation. You start in an area of sporadic
settlement, with stone foundations of clustered
huts and traces of early cultivation on the
hillsides. Later the foothills have hillforts, built
by incoming Celtic peoples and finally you
arrive at Powburn where the A697 road overlies the Devil's Causeway, a Roman Road.

    The route is hilly, but with moderate inclines.
It is 8.6 miles (13.7 km.) and can be walked
in about 4 or 5 hours. There are permanent
wet, muddy places, so stout footwear is recommended. Hartside has no public transport, but
Powburn is on a main bus route.

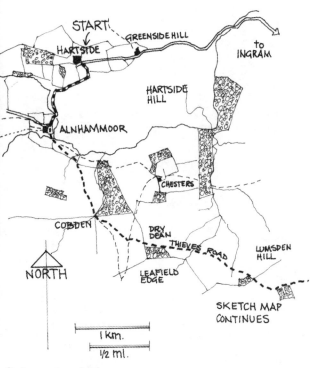

START
HARTSIDE
GREENSIDE HILL
to INGRAM
HARTSIDE HILL
ALNHAMMOOR
CHESTERS
COBDEN
DRY DEAN
THIEVES ROAD
LUMSDEN HILL
LEAFIELD EDGE
SKETCH MAP CONTINUES

NORTH

1 Km.
1/2 ml.

Cobden

From the road junction, just before Hartside,
take the metalled road South, finger-post-Alnham
Moor-1/2, down to the River Breamish and Alnhammoor just beyond. Hartside Hill, which you pass
on the left, has traces of early homesteads
and there are rig and furrow traces to the north
of Alnhammoor.

About 200 yards after crossing the river
and at the top of a rise, just before the farm
buildings, are two small wooden gates, with
waymarks, either side of a small field. From
the second gate bear left and shortly pass
through a metal farm-gate before crossing
over the Shank Burn by a wooden bridge to
a stile and a second metal farm-gate into a
riverside meadow.

Cross the meadow, bearing right, making

for a waymarked stile and a wooden farm-gate
onto a well-defined track rising beyond. Continue
heading uphill on the rutted track keeping the fence
on the left for part of the way to the corner of
a wood on the skyline at Cobden. At the wood
cross the Cobden Burn at the ford to the waymarked
stile next to a wooden farm-gate.

From Cobden continue uphill on a waymarked
grassy track across the moors, making for a line of
trees on the horizon and a metal farm-gate
situated at the start of the Thieves Road. The
Border troubles would appear to have given rise
to this name, as reivers would use it as a quick
route for their "lifted" stock back over the Border.
The Thieves Road connects with Salter's Road.
Many of the Border streets were also used as
trading routes, but they probably initially
connected Celtic settlements on either side of
the Border Ridge.

Whilst heading eastwards along the grassy
track of Thieves Road, between Leafield Edge
and Dry Dean, excellent views can be seen
of the surrounding hills, including Hedgehope
and the Cheviot. Eventually, after crossing
a small burn and passing through a couple
of metal farm-gates the Thieves Road
Plantation is reached. From here head
gently downhill to pass through a metal farm-
gate, then immediately climb the stile on
the left before continuing downhill eastwards,
making for the corner of a plantation about
200 yards ahead.

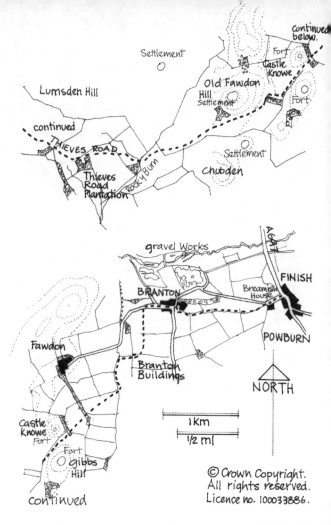

Settlement

continued below.

Fort

Castle Knowe

Old Fawdon Hill Settlement

Fort

Lumsden Hill

continued

THIEVES ROAD

Thieves Road Plantation

Rocky Burn

Settlement

Chubden

gravel Works

A697

BRANTON

FINISH

Breamish House

POWBURN

Fawdon

Branton Buildings

NORTH

Castle Knowe Fort

Fort

gibbs Hill

continued

1 km

1/2 ml

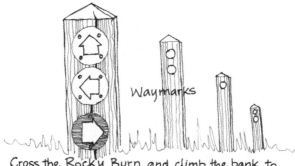

Waymarks

Cross the Rocky Burn and climb the bank to
pass through a metal farm gate, then immediately
turn left and go through a second metal gate to
head uphill across the meadow to a waymarked
wooden gate. The grassy footpath is well defined
and waymarked as it goes up round the north
side of Chubden Hill and over moorland. In summer
and autumn the path can become less obvious when
bracken is waist high. It is then best to head for the
'Y' shaped plantation just before Old Fawdon Hill.
The area in front of this plantation is often running
in water and boggy, the path is not very obvious.

A clearly defined settlement can be seen on
the right and there are hill-top forts on Old Fawdon
Hill, Gibbs Hill and Castle Knowe.

After about 600 yards a rectangular plantation
is reached through which, according to the O.S. map,
the footpath to Branton passes, but it is
indistinguishable in the trees. At present an
alternative route goes through a metal farm-gate
into a field at the left-hand corner of the wood,

waymarked "recommended path". Cross the field to the far gate avoiding a wet area by keeping near the wood until well past, then go back on to the track, a right of way.

This waymarked track passes between Gibbs Hill and Castle Knowe to a gap in a narrow woodland strip and a farm gate, which is often surrounded in mud.

From the top of the rise in the next field make for a gap in a second woodland strip directly ahead. Once through the wood and over the road leading right to Clinch, enter the field opposite and head downhill to the stile in the bottom left-hand corner of the field. Then cross a second stile into the next field. Turn left and, keeping the fence on the left, contour round Dun's Knowe, on the right, to a double metal farm-gate and out onto the drive leading up to Branton Buildings on the right.

Just before the buildings, at the top of the drive, go through two farm gates on the left and follow the waymarked route round behind the north side of Branton Buildings, bearing left to a fence ahead.

farm entrance, Branton.

this way

82

gate protruding from
the hedge

Keeping the fence on the right, head north through two fields and a small wooden gate, past the low rise of Cow Hill, to reach a wooden gate just before dropping down to the road. Finger post pointing back – Clinch 1, great Ryle 2½.

Once on the road head east through Branton village to a wide farmyard entrance directly ahead, on a bend. Ignore the right-hand turning to Glanton. Following the direction indicated by the fingerpost on the left enter the farmyard, turning immediately to the right, heading for a wooden farm-gate into a small field. In the field bear left immediately, keeping the house and a stone wall on the left and make for a waymarked stile into the next field.

After a short distance go through a metal farm-gate into the next field heading for a metal gate protruding from the hedge line. Keep heading eastwards, but now with the fence on the right.

Ignoring a footpath to the left, make for the next
gate ahead and follow the distinct grassy track
down to a gate and on to the road by Breamish
House. Fingerpost pointing back - Branton East Side
and the Clinch.

A short distance up the road brings you to
the A697 and Powburn. It also lands you on
the line of the Devil's Causeway, a Roman road
which branches off from Dere Street at Hadrian's
Wall and heads north, east of the Cheviots,
heading for the mouth of the Tweed.

Powburn is a village with all amenities.

Walk eight Powburn to Ellingham

Coming through Beanley

Having wound its way over the Cheviots the Borough boundary continues eastwards to the sea. Walk eight takes you over the Sandstone Ridge which divides the low lying land at the foot of the Cheviots from the coastal plain.

It is 12 miles (19 km) of easy walking and should take 6 or 7 hours. There are facilities at the start and finish, but nothing in between. If the weather turns really foul there are two escape routes.

Start on the north side of the bridge, opposite the unsigned road (where walk seven finished) and take the public footpath which follows the Pow Burn and woodland edge. (Kingfisher seen here.) On reaching the road to Beanley turn right and walk on for about 1/4 mile to a gate and fingerpost on the left, marked Low Hedgeley. The gravel pits on your left are being landscaped into lakes with islands and are already attracting many species of water birds.

Go through the gate and follow a clear track which skirts round the left edge of a wood, through another gate, ignoring the DEFRA path on your left. At the next gate turn right and follow the fence to a small burn. Cross the burn through the ford or over the log bridge and continue uphill, passing through a gate with Gamekeeper's Cottage on your right.

map continues

Harehope Farm

B6346

Great Wood

Gamekeeper's Cottage

Beanley

Hedgeley Hall

A697

Powburn

START

Keep on the track and up to the road. Turn left and continue along the road through Beanley until you reach a bend with a finger-post on the left signed Eglingham Cottage 1¼. Take this footpath, keeping the fence on your left and passing through a gate

87

until you reach a waymarked gate in the fence. Go through and cross the corner of the field diagonally, over a small burn, to a stile. Keep in the same direction, passing through some hawthorn trees and up to a fence. There is no obvious track here and the ground can be boggy. Follow the direction of the marker, keeping the fence on your right, to a gate. (Look out for deer.) The path here can get very overgrown in summer. Pass through the gate, turn immediately left and through another gate into the Great Wood and its magnificent old beech trees. At the end of the path through the wood turn right through a gate and follow the track to the end of the trees. Here, go half left and take the footpath across the field to a stile in the fence opposite. Cross over and walk through the trees to another stile. Over this turn right and go on to a gate which brings you out onto the Eglingham Road (B6346)

leaving Harehope Farm.

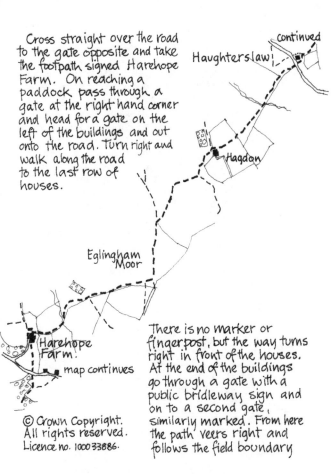

Cross straight over the road to the gate opposite and take the footpath signed Harehope Farm. On reaching a paddock pass through a gate at the right hand corner and head for a gate on the left of the buildings and out onto the road. Turn right and walk along the road to the last row of houses.

continued

Haughterslaw

Hagdon

Eglingham Moor

Harehope Farm

map continues

There is no marker or fingerpost, but the way turns right in front of the houses. At the end of the buildings go through a gate with a public bridleway sign and on to a second gate, similarly marked. From here the path veers right and follows the field boundary to a footbridge with another gate beyond. (Entering access land here.) The path is quite clear, going left before bending right through gorse bushes and bringing you to a small plantation on your left. At a large boulder on the left turn half right towards a wall and walk parallel to it up to Eglingham Moor. Continue until you reach a broad farm track signed Quarry House 2½m. Turn left onto the track. You are now on the Sandstone Ridge. The gently rolling heather moorland overlies fell sandstone, which has provided building material for many of the houses in the Borough.

On reaching a cattle grid ignore the bridle path on the left and continue on the stony track, going right, till you reach the farm at Hagdon. Immediately before the buildings turn left and make your way round to a stile. Cross this and keeping a fence on your right walk away from the farm.

Haughterslaw

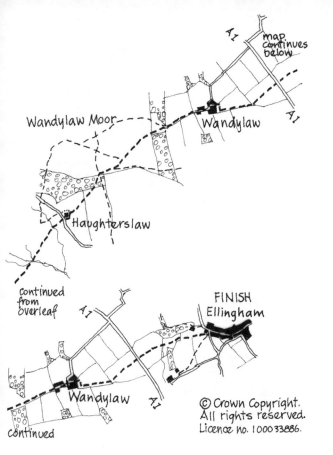

A1

map.
continues
below

Wandylaw Moor

Wandylaw

A1

Haughterslaw

continued
from
overleaf

A1

FINISH
Ellingham

Wandylaw

A1

Continued

© Crown Copyright.
All rights reserved.
Licence no. 100033886.

approaching Wandylaw

Pass through a gate following a line of telegraph poles and cross over a small stream as you approach Haughterslaw, which you can see in the distance.

On reaching the road from North Charlton turn left and walk on a few yards to a bridleway on the right, signed Wandylaw 1½ m. Follow this past the buildings to a gate. Once through go half right to another gate and continue on to a third by some gorse bushes.

(A diversion is planned at Haughterslaw as follows. Continue on the road past the farm to a gate on the right, beyond the last building. Go through and alongside the building, following the track to another gate by the gorse bushes. The diversion will be well marked.)

Keeping the gorse bushes on your left go up to a wood. Enter the wood and on emerging at the other end turn half right to pick up a track which heads to the left of another wood, which can be seen on the skyline.

At a gate follow the direction of the marker arrow onto a track which leads to a gap between two blocks of woodland. For a short way the path immediately after the gate is indistinct.   Go through another gate and continue on the track to Wandylaw, which can be seen straight ahead.

A diversion is planned at the farm, which will be well signed. At present this is the route. Where the road bends to the left, go straight ahead through the farm steading, as indicated by the fingerpost – Ellingham 1½ miles – ignore the road to the left. At the end of the buildings turn right by the yellow waymark and walk on for a short distance before turning sharp left, keeping the field boundary on your right. Where the path meets a gravel track cross over and take the footpath straight ahead down the field to the A1 road.

Cross with EXTREME CARE to the footpath opposite and continue over the field to a stile. Cross this and follow the track through gorse bushes and over a plank bridge to a gate. Pass through and follow the track down to Ellingham and the end of the walk – where the Packhorse Inn may be open.

Pack Horse Inn

walk nine
Ellingham to Seahouses

Ellingham
church
lychgate

This walk takes you from Ellingham through the pastoral coastal plain to Beadnell, then up the coast to Seahouses. The route wanders and twists because the rights of way round Beadnell don't run east and west. In spite of this the walk offers gentle going in peaceful country.

It is 11 miles (17·7 km), generally flat but boots are advised for fording the beach stream. There are limited facilities and no public transport at Ellingham, but Seahouses has everything, and funny hats too. If you walk on the beach be aware of the rise or fall of the tide and be careful on slippery rocks.

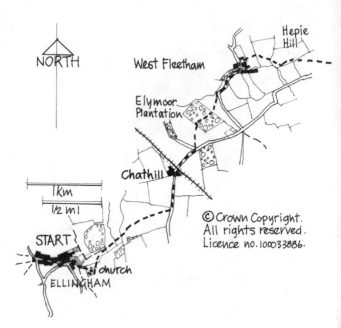

NORTH

West Fleetham

Hepie Hill

Elymoor Plantation

Chathill

1 Km
1/2 ml

START

church

ELLINGHAM

From the Pack Horse Inn go east along the road to a T junction. Go left, keeping straight on where the main road bends right. Walk up to the church, ignoring a finger post on the left, go through the lychgate and round behind the church to find a narrow path stepping down through trees to a footbridge and gate.

Bear right over a tussocky field to a gate and stile in the wall. Keep straight on crossing the footbridge over the Long Nanny, climb the bank and follow the line of telephone poles through a long field to a gate in the left-hand corner.

Go onto the road walking left to Chathill. The station is on the main East Coast line, with two trains stopping each way daily. The waiting room has information on local railway history.

Follow the B1340 road over the level crossing and past a large house to a farm track on the left with a fingerpost - public footpath, West Fleetham, 1. A wicket gate on the right leads to a large field. Aim for a gate half way along Elymoor Plantation, beneath a large oak tree.

In the wood go sharp left, then sharp right, following the path which is obstructed towards the far end. Find your way to the fence, walking right to a broken wicket gate.

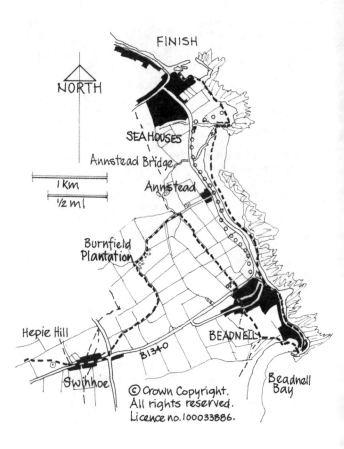

FINISH

NORTH

1 Km
½ ml

SEAHOUSES

Annstead Bridge

Annstead

Burnfield
Plantation

Hepie Hill

BEADNELL

B1340

Swinhoe

Beadnell
Bay

Chathill post office

Cross the cultivated field bearing half left to a clump of trees. Behind a large beech is a wicket gate. Ignore the fingerpost and go right to the road, walking left to West Fleetham. At the end of the hamlet you approach terraced cottages, end on to the road. A fingerpost on the right— public footpath, Swinhoe, 1 - directs you along in front of the houses to a stile.

Keep on through two gates then bear half right to a stile in the fence opposite. Go right following the field edge on your right. Just past a field entrance a stile brings you to a large field with traces of rig and furrow ploughing.

Aim to the left of trees round a pond and keep on towards Swinhoe and a gate in the right corner leading onto the road. Walk up past Swinhoe. The road is busy but rights of way through the farm are blocked, so this is the only option.

~approaching Swinhoe

At the cross roads go left for a short distance
to a farm gate on the right with a fingerpost-
public footpath, Annstead, 1¾. Cross the field
diagonally to a gate in the left hand corner,
go through, following the hedge on your left
to a wide gate where the hedge is on your right.
Follow the hedge, curving round to the left to
a stile in a wall. Continue towards Burnfield
Plantation on the right finding a wicket gate
below chestnut trees. Follow the grassy path as
it gradually bears left to reach a gate giving
onto a farm road.

Ignore the right-hand road and keep on
towards Annstead Farm looking out for
waymarked double gates on the right.

At this point the walk can be shortened by
continuing through Annstead to the coast
and walking left to Seahouses.

Otherwise go right at the gates following
the field wall on your right to a gate where
the path crosses to the other side of the wall.
Walk on to a stile, then cross another three fields
and stiles, all in the same direction. A final
stile brings you to a narrow tree strip and a

wooden stile delivers you
on to the busy coast road.
Cross carefully, going
right for 200 yards, then
left into Beadnell. Walk
through to a T junction
and a gated footpath
beyond, fingerpost -
Lime Kilns and Harbour.
Walk down to the caravan
park and follow its road left to a large carpark.
Cross it to a gap in the sand dunes and go
along the beach to the harbour.

gable in Beadnell

Beadnell Bay stretches away south with the
Borough boundary running out half way
down, with the Long Nanny. You are now in the
Northumberland Coast Area of Outstanding
Natural Beauty which stretches almost to
Berwick.

Beadnell Harbour

From the harbour go left from the Kilns, past the turreted house, then left again following the road through the village to its junction with the coast road. (ice cream) There is a choice of routes here. The newly opened Coast Path crosses the road and makes its way through the camp site and continues through fields. At the third field it crosses diagonally to a stile and fingerpost  on the coast road. The route then follows the road verge past Seahouses golf clubhouse turning right at the  sign, where it crosses the golf course turning left at the coast to arrive in Seahouses.

Alternatively you can find your way from the road junction through the dunes to the beach if tide conditions are suitable and walk round Annstead Bay to Seahouses.

At the north end of the beach Annstead Burn runs out to the sea. Usually it is a mere trickle but if not go up to the road and over Annstead Bridge.

Fording the burn continue to the sea end of low cliffs where a narrow path leads up to the golf course. Be careful crossing the rocks because they can be slippery.

Cross the golf course on the waymarked path. Look out for flying golf balls. The Coast Route joins from the left and both routes continue to arrive above Seahouses harbour.

Seahouses harbour

walk ten
Seahouses to Belford

Monks House

Walk ten takes you along stretches of 'Northumbria's Lordly Strand', past the capital of Anglo Saxon Northumbria and inland to Belford. It is a walk of 9 miles (15km) and should take 4 to 5 hours on easy terrain. There is public transport at both ends and facilities at Seahouses, Bamburgh and Belford.

From the centre of Seahouses walk north, taking the road to Bamburgh. At the northern end of the village, where the houses end, find a path to the right, through the dunes on to St. Aidan's Bay and proceed up the beach.

Shortly to your left you will see a group of houses hugging the shore – Monk's House. A stream comes out onto the sand, but it is shallow and easily forded. Later Bamburgh Castle comes into view. It was the capital of the Kingdom of Anglo Saxon Northumbria and the centre of the great cutural flowering known as the Golden Age of Northumbria.

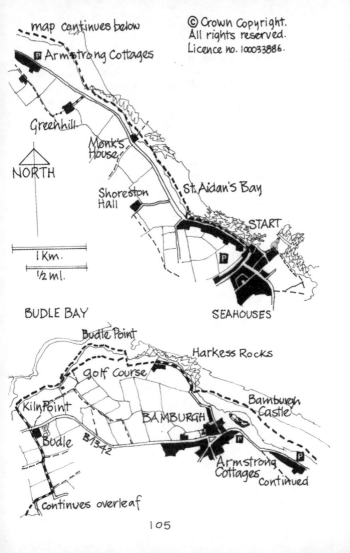

map continues below

P Armstrong Cottages

Greenhill

Monk's House

NORTH

Shoreston Hall

St. Aidan's Bay

1 Km.
½ ml.

START

P

BUDLE BAY

SEAHOUSES

Budle Point

Harkess Rocks

Golf Course

Kiln Point

Bamburgh Castle

BAMBURGH

Budle

B1342

P

Armstrong Cottages

P

Continued

continues overleaf

Walk on beyond the castle towards the Harkess Rocks. Veer left and climb to the road, turning right, heading for the lighthouse and walking to the Golf Club House on your left. Fingerpost-Coast Path, public bridleway, Budle Point, 3/4.

Here you have a choice. If the tide is well out go down onto the beach and follow it round into Budle Bay with Budle Point on your left. This is the southern limit of the Lindisfarne Nature Reserve. However, if the tide is high follow the right of way, marked with short blue posts, across the golf course, avoiding flying golf balls. Descend through the dunes, heading north-west down towards the shore ignoring a waymark pointing to the left. Follow the shore line round to Kiln Point where you will see a Nature Reserve notice. Budle Bay is a vast stretch of mud flats and salt marsh at low tide. It is a bird watcher's paradise.

At this point turn left on to a grassy track, past cottages on your right, up to the B1342 road.

Bamburgh Castle

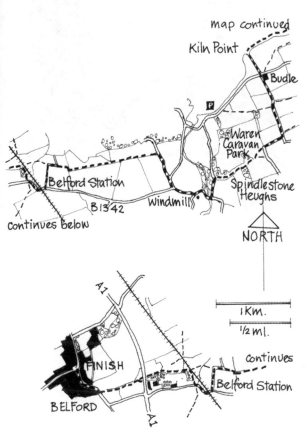

map continued
Kiln Point
Budle
P
Waren Caravan Park
Belford Station
B1342
Windmill
Spindlestone Heughs
Continues below
NORTH

A1
FINISH
BELFORD
A1
1 Km.
1/2 ml.
continues
Belford Station

Spindlestone Mill

Cross over the road, taking the minor road opposite, passing some recently refurbished farm buildings, now luxury homes. Ignore fingerposts to left and right and after about 1/3 mile turn right into a road leading to Waren Caravan Park. As you approach the entrance a fingerpost— public footpath, Spindlestone Mill, 3/4 — directs you through the site to a new wicket gate in the bottom corner and into a field. Go right, through a small wood and two fields and enter woodland on your right. Descend through the trees with Spindlestone Heughs up to the right. This was the setting for the ballad of the Laidley Worm.

"Word went east and word went west
   Word is gone over the sea
That a Laidley worm in Spindleston Heugh
   Would ruin the North Countree."

The giant worm was really a princess from Bamburgh Castle, transformed by her wicked stepmother, but restored by her brother with three kisses.

Coming down onto the road go left to a T junction at a dilapidated mill.

Turn right at the junction and cross the bridge, then climb the hill towards a windmill on the left. Ignore a road coming in from the left and carry on to the B1342. You will see a finger-post for the Coastal Path – *N* – directing you right and after 100 yards another finger directing you up a minor road where the main road curves right.

A short distance along the minor road a fingerpost on the left – *N*, public footpath, Station Cottages, 1½, Belford, 2½ – directs you along three fields with rising land on your right. At the end of the third field follow the signs right, then almost immediately left across a field to a gate leading onto a stone track. You are approaching the main east coast railway line. It is safest to turn left, following the track down to the B1342, emerging at whitewashed cottages.

the windmill

the track past the grain silos

Turn right, pass a row of stone cottages and cross the gated level crossing. You will walk on the pavement past the former station. Ahead is a row of brick cottages with a fingerpost just beyond - Public Footpath - Belford 1 - go straight up the stone track, past grain silos on your left, then go left to find a stile and a path leading along the back of more silos on the left.

The path soon reaches the A1 road. CROSS WITH CARE, via the stiles and follow the directions towards Belford with the golf course on your right and its driving range on your left. The path emerges onto the golf club car park. The village lies ahead. Taking a right turn at the golf club gates go along High Street to the village cross and the Blue Bell Inn.

Belford to Holy Island Causeway
Walk Eleven

Walk eleven is an easy 7 miles (11 km) on road, paths and tracks. Short lengths of path can become overgrown in summer and the busy A1 road must be crossed carefully.

Belford has a regular bus service to and from Berwick and Newcastle. A notice on the former bank in the village centre indicates that there are a church, pubs, post office, shops and public toilets.

Start from the market cross, opposite the Blue Bell, an old coaching inn, and walk uphill with the church on your left and the post office on your right. The road was formerly the A1, but the bypass has transformed it into a quiet country lane. In the reign of Charles I, Belford was described as "the most miserable beggardly town of sods that ever was made in an afternoon, of loam and sticks." Things have improved since then.

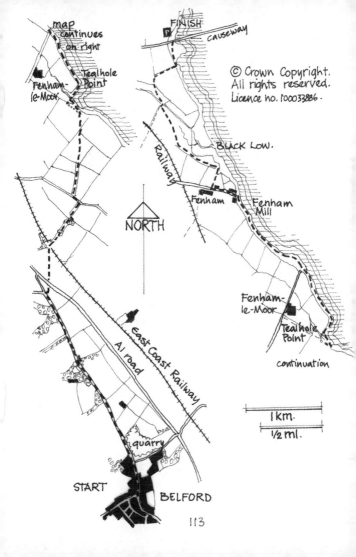

map continues on right

FINISH

causeway

Fenham-le-Moor

Tealhole Point

BLACK LOW.

Railway

Fenham

Fenham Mill

NORTH

Fenham-le-Moor

Tealhole Point

continuation

East Coast Railway

A1 road

quarry

START

BELFORD

1 km.

½ ml.

113

There is a pavement all along the road, but it changes sides occasionally. Cragmill Quarry, on your right, produces crushed whinstone aggregate. Further on, the neo-gothic gateway to Middleton Hall, lies on your left. There are good views of Lindisfarne, the busy A.1 and the East Coast Railway. The wood on the left is thickly carpeted with bluebells in May.

After 1·8 miles (3km) take a track opposite the road to Detchant. Fingerpost- Public Byway. The track soon arrives downhill at the A1 CROSS CAREFULLY (a couple of minutes spent waiting for a gap in the traffic is time well spent). The path continues to a stone bridge over the railway, then through Railway Plantation with Kettle Burn alongside on the left.

the bridge over Foulwork Burn.

About ¼ ml. after the railway bridge look out for a wooden footbridge on the left. Cross the stream, go left for a few yards, then right through a metal farm gate into a broad grassy path between thorn hedges, continuing in a north easterly direction.

At the path end go through a metal gate on to the road. Go left and very soon turn right at metal gates. Fingerpost- Public Bridleway - Fenham-le-Moor. 1¼ ml. Follow the bridleway north-north-east coming into a grass field. Holy Island can be seen straight ahead across Fenham Flats. Pass through a wicket gate and continue on the same line through the next field to reach the shore.

There are alternative routes for a short distance. Firstly go down to the foreshore, following round the high tide line to a high footbridge over Foulwork Burn.

Secondly, if the tide is very high, continue along the edge of the field, then turn right on to the footbridge.

The tidal mud flats are host to many birds, such as visiting Brent and Greylag geese which feed on the abundant inter-tidal plants.

Cross the burn keeping straight on along the shore line to Tealhole Point, where the path goes north-west past a black hut, a posh weekend cabin and a two storey hide at the end of the road from Fenham-le-Moor. Continue along the shore with a choice of grass path or gravel beach. Pass close to Fenham Mill, with the path becoming muddy, but reaching a large yellow notice board just beyond a private slipway. English Nature provides information and byelaws for the Lindisfarne Nature Reserve. Go up a short path between trees behind the notice board, arriving on the road. Continue towards Fenham, passing houses on your right and opposite farm buildings turn right on to a path. Fingerpost - Holy Island Causeway - 1½ ml.

the two storey hide

Fenham Mill

Go through a metal farm gate, bearing left, round a large stone barn and continuing with a fence and hedge on your left. At the end of the rather swampy field there is a stile on the left where St. Cuthbert's Way joins our route. Ignore it and find a stile on your right. Cross a small bridge over Beal Cast and another stile. Now, following St. Cuthbert's Way, cross the next field diagonally to a wide gap in the hedge with a metal gate. A wide path, fenced on both sides, soon brings you to a footpath on the right leading to a new wicket gate and the foreshore. Turn left, walking between huge concrete blocks, the remains of W.W.2. defences, to reach the Holy Island Causeway. The walk ends at the car park.

A bus service operates between Berwick and Holy Island, but it is tide-dependent, so times vary.

If you have time and the tide is right (see table of safe crossing times) a visit to the island is recommended.

Holy Island Causeway to Berwick
walk twelve

the path from the causeway

The twelfth and final section of the walk round Berwick Borough starts at the Holy Island Causeway and follows the coast up to the starting point at Berwick. There are tracks and minor roads along the coast and when the tide is low golden sands make easy walking, however care should be taken at Cheswick and Cocklawburn where slippery shelving ridges of rock run out to sea. Even more care should be taken at Goswick where notices warn of quicksands and unexploded bombs!

The walk is 10 miles (16 km.) and it can be walked in about 5 hours. There are no facilities until you reach Spittal.

From the car park at the causeway walk north between the concrete blocks of W.W.2. defences. You are now following the newly created Coastal Path, part of the developing pan-European North Sea Trail, with its distinctive logo, 'N'.

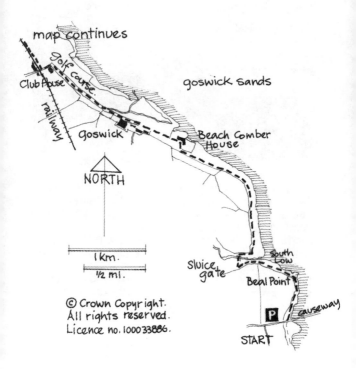

map continues

golf course

Club House

railway

goswick

goswick sands

Beach Comber House

NORTH

1 km.

½ ml.

Sluice gate

South Low

Beal Point

P

causeway

START

Beyond the blocks continue along the shore, turning left round Beal Point. The public right of way actually runs on top of the low cliffs, but there are unprotected trenches in the long grass and the safest policy is to keep to the shore.

Continue up the South Low, now on grass, towards the sluice gates in the distance, keeping alongside the fence on your left. Go up the grassy bank turning right along a gravel path to the Beal Sluice. Go through two wicket gates and follow more gravel path as it swings right.

The track reverts to grass following the coast inside the dunes, with broad views and skylarks serenading your progress. There are two gates across the way near Beachcomber House,

a former salmon fishing station, with a war-time observation tower. The track becomes a rough stony road as it swings right then left round the buildings. Continue along the straight road, passing Coastguard Cottage on your right and Goswick Farm on your left.

Beal Sluice

Goswick Farm

An old local rhyme explains that mainland farms supplied Lindisfarne Priory with food—
"From Goswick we've geese, from Cheswick we've cheese;
From Buckton we've venison in store;
From Swinhoe we've bacon, but the Scots have it taken,
And the prior is longing for more."
As the road becomes public it passes the links of Goswick Golf Club. Pass the clubhouse and go left with the road towards the railway. Turn right just before the level crossing (fingerpost, Coastal Path) following the railway fence on your left. At the end of the field go right for a short distance, turning left though a kissing gate and shortly through another kissing gate to join a grass track straight ahead running parallel to the fence on your left.

At the Cheswick road end go straight on through two metal gates to follow a gravel path. You will reach a gate marked "Private Land", with a stile alongside. On the left is a pond with fishing stages. To the right the fields

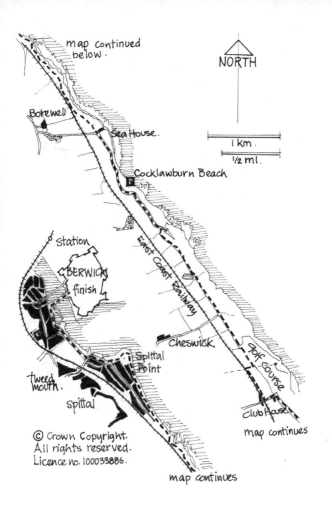

map continued below.

NORTH

1 km.
½ ml.

Borewell

Sea House.

Cocklawburn Beach

East Coast Railway

Station

BERWICK
finish

Cheswick

Golf Course

Spittal
Point

Tweed
mouth.

Spittal

Club House

map continues

map continues

are full of wild flowers, particularly cowslip and bloody cranesbill. A prominent mound appears ahead - an old lime kiln with ramped access from the south and a W.W.2. concrete pill box on top. The path arrives at twin gates and bends right to meet the road. Go left following the road to Cocklawburn Beach, a popular summer playground. Beyond the beach are cliffs which stretch all the way to Spittal. In the distance is the distinctive silhouette of Sea House.

Follow the road uphill, over a cattle grid, to Sea House, where it goes left to a railway crossing. Your route continues straight on, Fingerpost - Public Byway, Spittal 1 3/4, Coast Path, . Go between wind-bent trees to another cattle grid with a wicket gate at the side.

The cliff top path leads on to Spittal with the railway never far away on the left and wide views over Berwick Bay. Ahead lies the exclamation mark of the lighthouse at the end of Berwick Pier. At a further cattle grid go through the wicket gate and in about 200 yards find steps going down to the right, to Spittal Promenade.

Cocklawburn Beach

Spittal Promenade

The prom was rebuilt recently as a heightened sea defence. Half way along, the Venetian Pavilion has refreshments and public conveniences round the back.

At the end of the prom your path goes round Spittal Point, where the old industrial buildings have mostly been demolished, leaving the tall brick chimney as a splendid landmark. From the car park on the point follow the road round to the left, crossing another car park diagonally to a stony road which comes out on to the main road.

Go right towards Tweedmouth and Berwick. You will now see Berwick across the River Tweed with its defensive walls and the three bridges.

The road passes the lifeboat station and the Carr Rock Jetty, then leads on to Tweedmouth Dock with a wide grass strip alongside. Pavements take over in Tweedmouth and at the end of Main Street the road bends right leading you on to Berwick Bridge, which was built in 1611–34 at the suggestion of James VI and I, when he came south to assume the English throne.

Across the bridge you arrive at Bridge End, your original starting point. There are seats where you can take a well-earned rest and there is a pub on the corner.

Notes

Also published by Berwick Ramblers
BERWICK WALKS
twenty-four walks within a twelve
mile radius of Berwick, written
and illustrated by Arthur Wood.
ISBN 0-9545331-0-0 (978-0-9545331-0-6)

Notes